THE SLEEPING GYPSY

AND OTHER POEMS

THE SLEEPING GYPSY

AND OTHER POEMS

BY GEORGE GARRETT

AUSTIN · UNIVERSITY OF TEXAS PRESS · 1958

PUBLISHED AS A SUPPLEMENT TO *The Texas Quarterly*, VOL. I NO. 2

LIBRARY OF CONGRESS CATALOG CARD NUMBER 58–10848

MANUFACTURED BY THE UNIVERSITY OF TEXAS PRINTING DIVISION

FOR SUSAN

ACKNOWLEDGEMENTS

TWENTY-ONE of the poems in this volume have either appeared or will shortly appear in the following publications: *Sewanee Review, Western Humanities Review, New Poems by American Poets No. 2* (Ballentine), *Approach, American Weave, College English, Epos* (and *Epos Anthology 1958*), *Four Quarters, Perspective, Prairie Schooner,* and *Coastlines Literary Magazine.* The author is grateful to the editors concerned for permission to include these poems in the present collection.

CONTENTS

vii

IV SHORT STORIES

I THE MUSIC OF THIS WORLD

Solitude, récif, étoile
A n'importe ce qui valut
Le blanc souci de notre toile.
          MALLARMÉ, *Salut*

THE SLEEPING GYPSY

A grammar will teach you how to sing
clause on clause and in the center
of the knotted thought the verb bring
home, prodigal in glory, supple tiger

in tame cage displayed. Let fables frame
in excellence their brutal laws.
Know eye and ear are liars, nothing name
that can't be conquered or be shamed.

Far from your dream, your fireside, sleeps
the gypsy, prowls the ungovernable lion.
A guitar is the sum of all its silence, keeps
nothing but music caged; and the wan

moon struggles to be free. This rage
for justice and anarchy of evocation
must be learned. See, like a blank page,
the desert is desire and desolation.

3

DISTANCES, DIFFERENCES

From a tower on the mountain top
we could see five states. They lay
in pools of green and brown and gray
like continents on a bright map

in two dimensions. We
saw them as we saw the land,
level and gentle as an open hand
with not one fist for boundary.

It seemed a kind of eloquence
to be so high and to look down
like angels on the shining lawn
of all that's earthly distance.

I was on a ship once and
fog closed in like a long sigh.
I couldn't see the sea or sky
and I was far from any land

I had a name for. Eyes
burned out from staring at the sun
must see all differences in one
such shade where facts and lies

like lion and lamb together
huddle in dreamy prayer.
I can love both—the high, keen air,
the ghostly breath of foggy weather.

Logic is something else, a truth
that's all the knotty clenching of
barbwire to shelter what we love,
barricades to keep our wrath.

BUZZARD

I've heard that holy madness is a state
not to be trifled with, not to be taken
lightly by jest or vow, by lover's token
or any green wreath for a public place. Flash
in the eyes of madmen precious fountains,
whose flesh is wholly thirst, insatiate.

I see this bird with grace begin to wheel,
glide in God's fingerprint, a whorl
of night, in light a thing burnt black,
unhurried. Somewhere something on its back
has caught his eye. Wide-winged he descends,
like angels, to the business of this world.

I've heard that saintly hermits, frail, obscene
in rags, slack-fleshed, with eyes like jewels, kneel
in dry sand, among the tortured mountains, feel
at last the torment of their prayers take shape,
take wings, assume the brutal rush of grace.
This bird comes then and picks those thin bones clean.

AUBADE

Let the marvels cradled by this morning grow,
green shoots, beanstalking into a land of knowing
giants who, bearded as Abraham, poor as sheep,
wait for arrivals and the final weeping⁓
      which will make them wise.

May morning, to fountain and to fairy tale
aspiring, wholly surviving all clanging
and alarms, become an image of unfailing
promises which, fertile, fruitful, hang
      gardens under skies

as clear and cold as silent bells. Praise
for the child, unknown avenger, who
wakes to climbing, climbs to raise
eyebrows in hell and, beautiful, the truth
      to shear of all sighs.

GIANT KILLER

I've heard the case for clarity. I know
much can be said for fountains and for certain bells
that seem to wring the richness from the day
like juice of sweetest fruits, say, plums and tangerines,
grapes and pineapples and peaches. There are so many
ripe things, crushed, will sing on the thrilled tongue.

I know the architecture of the snow's composed
of multitudes of mirrors whose strict forms
prove nothing if they do not teach that God loves all
things classic, balanced and austere in grace
as, say, Tallchief in Swan Lake, a white thing floating
like the feather of a careless angel, dropped.

But there are certain of God's homely creatures that
I can love no less—the shiny toad, a fine hog fat in mud,
sporting like Romans at the baths, a mockingbird
whose true song is like oboes out of tune, a crow
who, cawing above a frozen winter field,
has just the note of satire and contempt.

I will agree that purity's a vital matter,
fit for philosophers and poets to doze upon. I'll agree
the blade is nobler than a rock. But then I think
of David with Goliath, how he knelt
and in a cloudy brook he felt for stones.
I like that disproportion. They were well thrown.

THE CHILDREN: AN ABSTRACTION

The children,
morning's parables, adapt
a whole day to their rapt
and various attention. The light,
as yet unbroken, burdens so

the day it swells, explodes
in symbols, and all roads
go straight and shining lead
nowhere but to home.

Choices
are simple in this atmosphere.
Forms are all classical and rear,
clean curve and angle, round and square,
an ample nakedness.

And light, light is everywhere
arranging, improvising, making clear
the contours of wishes, the careers
of least and lost things calling

to begin again. The children, holy fables
on this fictitious day, are fully able
to endure its failing though, prodigal,
the light is spent, the world is torn in two.

A FORM OF JOY

You have to learn the way
the cat, say, or the snake, the hawk,
all triggered, coiled or poised,
yet can be lax with waiting like
a bowstring, gutstring, or
the hangman's neat and empty noose.

You know a tale of cat and mouse.
You've watched a snake retreat
subtly on himself, head up, forked tongue
testing the air like a little flame.
You've seen a hawk hang high
on the lucid edges of the wind.

And then you've felt a kind
of chilly blur, furred or feathered,
trim with suppleness, whereby
claw and jaw, fang and talon
fall to seize a form of joy
utterly beyond telling.

In cloudy rigor silent bells
call for your hands to bruise
them into bursting song. So
dances the vacant noose, so strung
is bow or violin to catch
your least touch and resound,

rejoice and startle all creation
with the fury and the beauty of
action struck from pure repose.
Prayer is poise, silence is holy noise.
Be still. Dreamy, the floating hawk
descends like angels to your need.

UNDERWORLD

You've seen coal miners coming up
for air, all in blackface like
no minstrel show comedian,
but bent over, seamed by the danger
and the darkness they must bear,
at once a badge and a wound.

Or maybe a diver on the deck,
his heavy helmet cast aside,
blinking in the hard bright light
where every breath's a gust of fire.
It's no laughing matter
to live in two strange worlds.

So it is with certain myths and dreams.
The songs of Orpheus never were the same
after he'd seen hell. They roused
nothing but rage and madness, yet,
after such vision and such loss,
who wouldn't change his tune?

Oh, you'll descend, all right,
dream into a fiery darkness or
stumble, awkward among the deep sea
shiftings, troubled by bones
and voiceless cries. And then
you wake and wonder what is real.

Better to come up grinning,
scrub the darkness off yourself,
wisecrack with the ordinary seamen,
unless, like a careless saint, you can
give your soul to God. And then
your flesh belongs to furies.

ADVICE TO AN AESTHETICIAN

Begin with the simple thing,
with, for example, the emotion,
neither expressed nor unexpressed,
hidden or exposed, the abstract,
the unattained, untenable—
the joy of the rose.

Now study it patiently.
Be patient as the matador—
philosopher awaiting the horns
of a dilemma. Be brave,
a tireless theologian
tracking God in his cave.

Beginning is discovery
that creation is a whim,
defined, refined, elaborate
perfection of accidents. So
the enterprise is following
patterns as they go

and come again, detecting
order in spontaneity.
The beautiful is the spontaneous
and unbelievable example—
the rose, its complex poise,
its ample and expected joys.

THE PURE BRUTALITIES OF CONTRAST

A weather turns from green to gray.
There's an odor of decay
in things you take to heart.
Emphatic changes ask all art

that you can master to endure.
One anxious to enjoy the pure
brutalities of contrast runs
the risk, all reticence undone,

an inner ghost set free, that fists
will bless what has been kissed
and curse replace the highest praise
with equal justice. One pays

in kind for love and hate
as if the two were separate
and purity could be defined,
as if in the complex design

there were a secret you could share,
as if by skill you learn to pair
the saint against the sinner,
the outer weather and the inner.

STILL LIFE

An old man at the window looking,
say, like a cloudy moon, his face
pressed round and flat against the cold
glass. Outside a frozen day. Below
he can see his footprints march off
like stout twins and disappear.

Make it late afternoon, the sky
gathering gray around the trees,
the trees a tingle of icy limbs and
supplication which to his mood evoke
the final state of heroes—
dark bones, bright armor, prayer.

Behind him an oak fire, restless
as a dog on a chain, growling of
unspoken possibilities, flickering warm
in the room with shadows like wishes.
But keep him from looking at
the room he knows, a sentence

paused on a dependent clause, a cup
with a slice of lemon bobbing gently
like a painted island in a lukewarm sea.
Let him be silly and human—
pity the twins who got lost in the snow,
sigh while the heroes pray and glitter.

PASTORAL

The ghosts of summer learn,
leaning from banks of shade,
how the flowing world, made
holy of breath and dust, turns

always and the seasons shine
like new coins and are spent.
This is a school of discontent
where children of the light define

against the steady tide of dark
the meaning of their banishment
and find on everything the mark
of flood or fire. Not innocent,

there Adam sweats, there Cain raises
a brood of stony hearts. There David,
who downed giants and sang praises,
weeps. There Job composes

the logic of long suffering.
And we, the swimmers, sing
of light and dark who know
so little of so much. Worlds go

and come again, and these waves pound
the living and the dying, leaving
each alone, submerged, fearing
to rise and be counted with the drowned.

OLD SAWS NO. 1

"A rolling stone gathers no moss."

This is the simple truth: e.g. the rock
of Sisyphus (so lichenless it gleams
like a bald man in the sun) it seems
will never have a moment on its back

to sigh and stretch and feel a fine
green growing like a handstitched lace
among the honored piles in public place.
Few of us can mellow like good wine,

age into some gracious Judgment Day,
in caves as nice as any Plato thought;
but, daily sold and daily bought,
are judged and juggled, roll away

as smooth and nude as grapes on vine.
Still, there's pleasure in the constant dance
of things. Many will sparkle and by chance
a lone stone like a diamond shine.

OLD SAWS NO. 2

"You can't make a silk purse out of a sow's ear."

On the contrary, it appears
that truth is always in disguise.
Take, for example, the careers
of gods in flesh, so camouflaged,

they blend into the texture of
our sweaty dreams of sweatless enterprise,
or those tall heroes who for love
fall on all fours and howl like cats

in heat. This proves the silk
can be converted, you surmise,
but not the negative. We milk
this world (says Wilbur) but we don't believe.

I say that, blest, all water turns to wine.
I say there's more than meets the eye
when Salome, veil by veil, her fine
clothes peels to the essential skin

and bones. There are two thieves.
One of them spits and shuts his eyes.
The other, seeing truth so naked, grieves
and finds himself in paradise.

OLD SAWS NO. 3

"You can't plant peach pits and grow pear trees."

A man is more than sum of all his deeds.

Say that the finest actions could be kept
like flowers pressed in pages, say that doom
is totalled from a column of calm figures,
the dark and light, the services and sins,

until there comes in fire a single answer,
ineffaceable and indisputable, what then?
There are heroes for whom horses wept
and stones, and how shall frail perfume

from antique flowers guard a noble gesture,
though multitudes of ghosts may haunt the tomb?
Grass grows rich where white Adonis stepped,
and from the bones of Orpheus, bright as pins,

poems sprout still like grain from quickened seeds.

THREE STUDIES OF AESOP

FOR RICHARD WILBUR

1. The donkey in the lion's skin

I take this tale to prove
much that we love and fear
is false when tried by speech,

for only the lion should roar,
as cooing becomes the dove
and a peach is a peach is a peach.

But those whom gestures move
to sail for unknown shores
or taste of fruit beyond their reach,

must take the donkey for
a wise beast and approve
what he was trying to teach.

2. The raven and the fox

As usual, the fox is right.
And flattery's a terrible swift sword
and vanity a wound that doesn't heal.

But what was (in truth) the case?
Wasn't the chance that once,
just once, the raven's voice

would be seized by a wonderful tune
worth any morsel of food
and the sight of a satisfied fox?

18

3. The tortoise and the hare

If standing at the finish line
wreathed in flowers and/or smiles
for newspapers is what
counts, the moral's fine.

If such Persistence is correct,
praise the spider and the ant.
Fiddling grasshoppers can't
please Æsop's Architect.

But God knows there's a place
for those who for pure joy
run and fall asleep
while solemn others win a race.

SAINTS

Not all of them must suffer. Some,
once spoken for, once chosen, sing
of flawless weather in a jewelled city
turning and burning in the sun.

St. Anthony saw nightmares, and a wheel
still gives a name to Catherine's agony.
St. Sebastian took his feathered glory
as a magnet draws slim files of steel.

Others we honor lived a while
in landscapes crueler than the moon.
They learned by heart the sirens' tune.
They knew the tiger's brightest smile.

The rest are called, not chosen, must
daily put on old armor and ride out
to meet the dragon. They love the songs
of joyous saints whose tongues are holy dust.

SPEAKING OF MINOR REVELATIONS

(DAVID & GOLIATH)

What could be virtue in a giant
is rashness in small boys. The point
beyond which childhood is
calamity is clearly marked.

The giant, standing like a bear,
must be astounded, raise a roar
of natural indignation or
tilt to laugh at the improbable.

So they must always meet that way,
be disciplined and neat as puppets.
So I must always praise,
with brutal innocence, the accidental.

He's lucky who dies laughing
in the light of it, who leaves
the deft philosophers to argue
that excess is illumination.

BE UNCORRUPTED ALL

Be uncorrupted all, uprooted quite
from gnarling, grasp and grope.
Be straightened like uncoiling rope
spun whistling over water clean as sight.

Move urgently to mooring. Small
is a shadow, neither monster nor
exactly twin, tugging your toes, sprawled
like a drowned man on the ocean floor

whom tempest and tirade can never reach
to stir to action, torment into song.
In darkness lean towards light. Beseech
new blossomings to happen and the strong

ship, wave-whipped, safely to arrive
in harbor where loves like bright leaves thrive.

22

AFTER BAD DREAMS

Let holy saints, now safely out
of skin and bones, arise in unison
to tip their hats and halos of pure light.
Let angels dip their wings in flight,
scattering brightness like confusion
of ice and snow. Let poor ghosts shout,

sinners and losers, gray as smoke,
notorious and nameless in this glint
of morning, shout hosanna.
In sleep I walked the desert. Manna
did not fall. I lusted for a hint
of water, tasted dust. A dirty joke

troubled my tongue when I tried to pray.
Now there's light enough to swim in
and every stone smells freshly baked.
I drink the wine of morning for my shadow's sake,
he who has suffered and must suffer once again,
who now falls victim to a perfect day.

II SONGS

NARCISSUS

Hunter in the lonely field,
figure of our primal grace,
all that seems, all that's real,
united, lead you in the chase.

The arrow of the heart is keen;
if your hand is steady, true,
reality and the fierce dream,
stricken, will be cut in two.

And triumphantly you pose
beside the victim of your aim
whose frozen features now disclose
the beast you hunted had your name.

SNOWMAN

A season of the heart can change
  South wind blow warm, north wind blow cold
and what was known be wholly strange
and what was new be old.

All wintered, I am made of snow
  Blow warm south wind, return in flame
and where I am I do not know
and what I've loved can't name.

Return south wind with holy fire.
  Bring green to leaf, bring fruit to bough,
bring birds to sing, turn crowd to choir
where there's no music now.

A season of the heart can turn.
  North wind cuts cruel on bone and brain.
In strictest weather heart must learn
to grope to song again.

HERMIT

Now on my lips all words grow stale.
 I'll sing good-bye a dozen ways.
My father's ghost is wan and pale.
I watch the clock and count the days.

Now on my tongue all names taste dust.
 I love the swan, his dying tune.
By hawk and handsaw, ought and must,
I'm troubled in December as in June.

Now in my throat a curse keeps house.
 Bless Orpheus, his bloody bones.
Rage is my lawless dreaded spouse.
I can turn sweet bread into stones.

I know a cure for total loss.
 Sing farewell night and hello day.
You nail your god upon a cross
and kneel and hear your new voice pray.

III SNAPSHOTS

There's some Peculiar in each leaf and grain,
Some unmark'd fibre, or some varying vein:
Shall only Man be taken in the gross?
Grant but as many sorts of Mind as Moss.

POPE, *Epistle to Cobham*

THE LION TAMER

The Lion Tamer
is announced by a fanfare
of cornets and agitated snare drums.
He appears, a brisk figure from
a water color, and meets our stare,
tiny, pale in the floodlight glare.

This part is comedy
which all of us accept.
The scarlet coat, the puppet bow,
the stiff mustachios, all endow
the moment with the properly inept
artifice. Otherwise we might have wept

for him, surmising,
foolishly enough, how much alone
he'll be and what a raging trial
by fury is prepared. A painted smile
rejects all pity from his brilliant zone.
He can turn lions and tigers into stone.

TUGBOAT

Blundering behind a white mustache,
a dated handlebar of foam, squat and emphatic,
(One thinks of Teddy Roosevelt, those decades,
and John L. Sullivan who, though he mixed
with shanty Irish taste his bourbon and champagne,
could lick any man in the house.)
graceless as a pelican on the ground,
crude as a jackknife in a realm of swords,
this boat has virtues of its own,
swaggers, not without reason, among
the liners unlikely as birthday cakes,
the ploughboy freighters in straight furrow,
and the lean warships gray as sharks.

Prodigal, the fine ships come and go
like knights to seek whatever dragon,
whatever damsel the dubious horizon hides.
Leaving; the tug's a damn nuisance like a dog
yapping at your heels. Go home! Go home!
Returning, you spy your grave retainer coming,
faithful behind his poor mustache. On land,
out of armor, dragons no more than creatures of dream,
at home, by fireside, to be forgotten.
But now, for one moment, you must say:
"What a miracle is simple duty done!
How crude, how comic, and how rare!"

TYGER

Graceful's not always good.
The tiger lives in bright prison.
Flesh is a windy sea.

Who hasn't drowned
in a fiery glance?

God made him so.
Like whales.

We add more stripes to him,
clench him with iron fingers.
Eyes are beaks and claws.

Who hasn't feasted
on his bitter heart?

God made us so.
Like fists.

His heaven has no name.
Though ours be blue as water,
both of us breathe dust.

Who hasn't wished
to trade his cell?

God made him.
So like flame.

FIRE ENGINE

The siren equals the imperative
        color in emphasis,
        squealing like a stuck heart
        (if hearts could squeal).

Meanwhile the bell is clean-voiced
        like light or logic,
        like the cloudless tones
        of pure ideas.

The riders are dressed like priests,
        perhaps, or chosen
        heroes from an awkward age
        of ritual inclination

and obscure motives. They
        are clinging tightly
        (like coined figures)
        in flat profile.

You're sentimental, my friend,
        to pity the phoenix
        they're racing to douse—
        the sparkling destination.

And I'm irresponsible, fascinated
        by all bleating, roars
        and the rare urgency
        of delicate control.

A PARABLE OF FOUR SOWERS

1.

She was a dazzle.
How her words flew!
Like strange birds.

Who could capture
the fury of their wings
or their fierce songs?

Where I've planted
nothing will grow.
Nothing prospers.

Let dark birds come
now and find me.
Pluck out my eyes.

2.

My joy was joyless.
Her bright smile was
a pair of shears.

So rare her flesh!
But at my touch
she turned to stone.

All I can harvest
is crop of bruises.
Mouthful of chaff.

Pity the hunter
whose bowstring is slack.
Limp arrows in quiver.

3.

My love was rich.
Golden her body.
Coins for her eyes.

My love was treasure.
I was a pirate.
Faulty the map.

For crown I wear
thorns. For bread
I taste fists.

Find me a willow.
I'll show that tree
how to bear fruit.

4.

My love lay fallow.
Dust on her lips.
Green in my eyes.

My love was sleeping.
I stormed her dream
like a tall tower.

My love's a garden.
Wild children grow
calm in her hands.

My love is holy.
It would be prayer
to praise her in words.

TIGHTROPE WALKER

A tightrope walker,
in particular the frivolous one
dressed outlandishly in a top hat
and tails, invites one to participate
in the artifice of courage.

A red-faced schoolboy
who, choking behind a necktie,
recited "Horatius at the Bridge,"
could only offer the bright swords in
a Nineteenth Century gilt frame.

His colleague, the adult
politician, faced the lightning
of flashcameras with a heavy metaphor.
One was aware of flags and dust
and stern gods overseeing.

And neither one pleased
me much. One is embarrassed
by the ponderous intimation
of spectacular excess without
a redeeming irony.

But here, following
band music and bareback riders, one
could be delighted with the primary
assumption, the initial escapade.
He tipped his hat

to gravity and seemed
to reel, drunken, on the taut wire.
It takes such genuine bravado to salute
a fundamental concept. It takes such wit
to share a danger.

VETERANS

"But if the cause be not good . . ."
—KING HENRY V, IV. i.

It was a young soldier in King Henry's army
standing by a small fire, warming his hands,
who called up the Judgment Day, that reveille
when all the dead fall in and stand a muster.
He was afraid. He didn't speak
of echelons of angels and the brilliant saints
in open ranks, dressed right and covered down,
but of the mangled, the terribly wounded,
the butchered, slaughtered, with filthy bandages
falling away from scars too cruel to believe.

And on that latter day they'd swarm
to point with stumps and canes and crutches,
calling for justice, all in tongues of fire,
and each would have his holy story heard.
His words danced like ghosts in the dark.
But not a word from veterans. It was cold,
the fire was near and real, and they were warm
for once. Stars burn, too, but they are far
away. They will sleep. They will eat,
and in the morning some of them will die.

Oh, on that Day they'll simply fall us out
at four a.m., field kit and heavy pack.
In the chill dark you stamp your feet and whisper
to the next man down. This will be a hike.
The Old Man's fuming. Lieutenants bark like dogs.
"Who's in charge here?" "Move out smartly there!"
We sigh, and then our boots fall on the road
in perfect unison and make a kind of song.
It was the King who prayed. It was
the veterans who fired his winning arrows.

40

RIDDLE MAN

Inconstant, he is moved
by least things most,
by present less than past,
by what has been than to be loved.

Fictive, he captures
more from hinting edge
than inmost eye of rage.
Can wink at glint of what is rare.

Improbable, he believes
when ought to doubt.
He pays a sullen debt
to dead when he owes most to live.

Foolish, he's laughed
when close to tears;
but has cropped bitter tares.
When world was grain has fed on chaff.

Unlikely, it is he
who aims for love.
But not from here will move,
who most in chains thinks he is free.

THE LUCKY

I think of some of these,
some of the golden ones with such
a shine they seem to wear
a magic cloak like health.

Let others gnash their teeth,
sweat to gain the Midas touch.
Let others, shirtless, bare
many wounds, their wealth,

and chew the sour bone of wrath
and dance their little jigs of fear
from neck to knocking knees,
know hunger's knotty clutch.

It's the lucky, like the meek,
the very brave, the fair,
who will inherit all the earth
can offer, rare or rich,

brimming with too much
ripeness. Let others stare
in mirrors, pray for death
and hang from lonely trees.

ROMANTIC

I've heard some jealous women say
that if your skin were cut away
and tacked upon a public wall
it would not please the eyes at all.

They say your bones are no great prize,
that hanging in the neutral breeze
your rig of ribs, your trim of thighs
would catch no fetching harmonies

but tinkle like a running mouse
over piano keys. They hold
that, stripped, your shabby soul
will whimper like a vacant house

you are so haunted. "Ask
her," they say, "if she'll unmask.
Let her shed beauty like winter trees.
Time will bring her to her knees."

Still, I must have you as you are,
all of a piece, beautiful and vain,
burning and freezing, near and far,
and all my joy and all my pain.

And if you live to scrub a floor
with prayer, to weep like a small ghost,
which of us will suffer more,
who will be wounded most?

NARCISSIST

She in her lonely sleep turns
away, and I in the same dream burn
and freeze. This is the trance
of Saint Anthony, the perplexing

fevers from the darkness freed
to take the weeping forms of need.
Now let shadows like long sorrows spring
to life. Let nonsense of dreams

seem plausible and each
image stutter into naked speech.
Christ! to return, return, return,
the road forking with familiar choices,

the persistent baffled streets
of lost cities, ever-vexing maze
of burning eyes and clenched fists,
traffic of tormented heartbeats. . . .

I want to be simple and classical,
to awake in swimming light and sing,
like a bloodless figure of pure stone,
the rhythm and the joy of everything.

SENSUALIST

I know the story of a man.
Lordly, he owned five horses,
each of a different shade and temperament.

From green glow of dawn to dark brim
of evening he rode them hard.
How his short crop flashed
drumming the sweaty shining of their flanks!

He was more cruel than January
in a vineyard.

He was happy as a toad
in the cool of a deep well,

inconstant as the chameleon,
thriving splendidly on light and breath.

Five frightened horses trampled him to death.

A FRIEND IN GRAY FLANNEL

Gaunt as a ghost and just as gray
is this tall man tired
with the tight unmentionable
ailments of nerves:
who has danced to music
seized from a leaf-sprinting wind,
who was moved by rhythms
snared from a shoeshine rag,
who has given up all gaiety.

I sympathize, but I should say:
"Look, man, I've even heard the dead
chuckling in strict coffins,
and once, passing a prison,
I listened to laughter escape."
Since this would be an outright lie,
I can only sympathize
with the gray, torn man.

Anyway, what can *you say to a ghost?*

46

THREE FROM THE ACADEMY

1. Professor of *Belles Lettres*

His book-lined study ought to be a TV set.
Some very nice first editions in alphabetical order
and himself fully armed by J. Press,
chainsmoking while he conducts a class—
"The Growth of National Consciousness in American Lit."

There's a picture window with a view
of barbered green lawn and a man with a lawn mower.
"Italians love to cut grass," his wife said.

Afterwards there is tea
during which he collects
the latest undergraduate slang
in an indexed notebook.

I do not know if he believes in anything
or has any love by which he lives,
but, over the shine of the teacups
and the glint of the silver service,

have seen tears in his eyes
when he talked about Sacco and Vanzetti
or the peace of Walden Pond.

2. Gadfly

At the Faculty Meeting I saw him bleed
for Nonconformity and, good classicist, bare
all his wounds, calling on us to rise, rebel,
to shrug the yoke, come down from bitter cross.

    The President, I noticed, was impassive,
    attentive and indifferent as a croupier.
    Not the least fault or fissure of emotion
    troubled the contours of his familiar smile.

Now this is Ancient History.
We live and learn.

The Gadfly was promoted while
Rebels were scattered like a covey of quail
in everywhich direction.
Folding their caps and gowns like Arab tents,
they muttered "tar and feathers," fled.

Now over coffee, steaming rich
subsistence of the academic nerve,
I hear him say: "What we need
is less of milk and honey and more sting.
Things hereabouts are whitewashed. Let us
act. A little water clears us of the deed.
    And what do you think?"

I smile and shrug.
I pay the check and plead a class
and leave him talking still,
safe in the shadow of his Great Man,
a trim Diogenes in tub of honest tweed.

3. Pedant

Privately, your pencil makes
wry marginalia, doodles at the edge
of noted pages, underlines examples of
what you call the worst excesses.

"Puddles of sentiment!" You scrawl
an epitaph for Shelley and his critics,
being uneasy among the vague Romantics.

"Pope & Swift would have admired
 Bentley & Dennis
if only they had understood."
Thus gladly reconcile and make a peace
among the factions of your favorite century.

If I hide my mouth to laugh,
if I yawn, doze while you drone,
if, choking on my imprecision,
I curse you in the language of those years
for "a Blockhead and a Fine Dull Ass,"
I must (in truth) confess

your strictness is like a conscience,
your rigor's like the pattern which
the feet must follow in numbered silence
before they waltz free to real music.

One learns to count before one learns the dance.
One learns to speak grammatically before
one takes the stance of satire and/or praise.

And I have seen the virtue of
your passion for precision.
You teach, by vehement revision,
that labor is a way to love.

SIR GUY OF GYSBANE*

FOR THE GRAD STUDENTS—PAST, PRESENT, FUTURE—AT PRINCETON

Springtime and the leaves like a green lace,
yet thick and warm as tongues calling his name,
when Sir Guy came at last into the strange country.

His armor was rusty, wore the scars of flame.
One eye was bloodshot, the other patched,
and if he smiled, his mouth was a ruined fence.

Nothing out of all his stern experience
popped (jack-in-the-box) to help him understand
what he was seeing—the horses gaunt, the men

as thin and quiet as shadows and
so broken, so crippled, so hurt,
that even he *felt oddly whole.*

There were sights there to break his heart
(that which has been called a thing of stone
by more than one gnashing set of teeth),

and now, tired out and all alone,
he felt bones trickle and blood go cold,
for first time ever knew the sweat of fear.

"What are you *doing here?"*
Cried a stranger on a sagging crutch.
But another offered him a wooden hand.

"Welcome, Sir Guy, to your native land.
Don't be afraid," he (smiling) said.
"We are all wounded in this place."

* This is, I hope, the only poem in the book that needs a note. Sir Guy of Gysbane is an imaginary Mediaeval figure—soldier, scholar, statesman—created by the gradgrinds, myself included, at Princeton. At first we used him to plague aging professors with oblique references to his canon and career. Later he was used, like a left-handed monkey wrench or a bucket of polka dot paint, to trouble the new students. They searched in vain for him in the dim stacks of the library. Finally, he became a symbol (perhaps Sisyphus would have been a more accurate one) for our labors. I've always liked Sir Guy. He had a certain dash and bravado even though his life was sad.

50

CAEDMON

All uncompelled, weightless as the notes
wrung out of bells at kindling dawn,
more light-thrilled than a shallow stream
over brute rock dashed, these thoughts
flash to song like figures from a dream.

Creation roars. Happens in fire and flood
the riot which is God. A flock of hurts
(the sad crowd, grazing of bitter hearts,
the blank gaze, fright in the rotten wood)
released, reprieved, departs

as, naked, empty as a broken bowl
of everything save light and air, I learn
to praise the water, praise the fire. Burns
then, eternal phoenix, all the soul
I was, and I rejoice to be reborn.

SWIFT

Swift has been misunderstood, his rage
called everything but honesty,
the buzzing in his brain identified
as everything but the lightning of God.

Now scholars nod over the burning page,
with pencils poised, fidget and warble
their footnotes wild, and Stella is
and she isn't, and God knows

Swift had marbles in his head—
tall sculptured figures posing there,
bright and naked, the image of
the rare and endless possibility of man.

Follow him, if you can, with eyes
wide open. Sketch for a skeptic age
the contours of his anger and his love.
Be humble if he, furious, replies.

TIRESIAS

Speak to us who
are also split.
Speak to the two
we love and hate.

You have been both
and you have known
the double truth
as, chaste, obscene,

you were the lover
and the loved.
You were the giver
who received.

Now tell us how
we can be one
another too.
Speak to us who

in single wrath
cannot be true
to life or death.
Blinder than you.

MARTHA GRAHAM: *APPALACHIAN SPRING*

*Our blue mountains are vague as smoke. In April we dream we
are awake. Our dreams are pink and white like dogwood and as sweet
as rock candy.*

*Then the Devil comes walking like a bear on his hind legs,
and his fiddler sets everything to dancing. O Martin Luther,
O Jack Calvin, can't you keep those tunes out of my ears? In
April, in May, the Devil makes his music like a fat bumblebee
in the flowers.*

Thank the Lord, the long dry summer days come soon after.

CLASSIC GENERALISSIMO

So, finally the emperor was fed up
with the shape of things. His statues in the park
leaned and slouched like beggars after dark.
Imagine that: equestrians with tin cups!

His ribbons wilted. His uniform came back
from the dry cleaner's faded and shrunk.
"Colossal anarchy! All government is bunk!"
Roared the dictaphone behind his back.

He stood up tiredly, buckled on his sword.
Thousands waited underneath his window,
thousands waiting for his final words.

He spoke briefly. "Goodness is enormous. War
is a grotesque dance, and life's a puppet show.
Where do all sweets go? How should I know?"

IV SHORT STORIES

SUMMER STORM

In such a wind the trees
toss their bright heads like women
in a pique of rage or disappointment.

In such a wind the clouds
go wild, stampede, dark and shaggy
as buffaloes and prophets.

"Whip me such honest knaves!"
Howls the professor, high-lighted,
theatrical behind his lawn mower,

amid the wink and crack of thunder
and lightning as the rain
comes flashing like a thousand swords,

like Agincourt's deft arrows.
His child, inside the house, looks
out. "The bears!" He cries.

"The grizzly bears are running away
with the sky!" He's delighted.
Not every day the zoo's turned loose.

The wife from her bedroom sees
the professor soaked and stamping.
Smiles. He never knows when

it's time to come out of the rain.
She tosses her hair like the trees,
shakes free her careful hair

and stands by the window in the dark room.
"Take me with you," she whispers
to the wind. "Let me go running

naked and young in the whips of rain.
Take me with you." (to the wind)
"I promise I'll be good."

THE MAGI

First they were stiff and gaudy,
three painted wooden figures on the table,
bowing in a manger without any walls
among bland clay beasts and shepherds
who huddled where my mother always put them
in a perfect ring around the Holy Child.
At that season and by candlelight
it was easy for a child to believe in them.

Later on I was one. I brought gold,
ascended the platform in the Parish House
and muffed my lines, but left my gift
beside the cheap doll in its cradle,
knelt in my fancy costume trying to look wise
while the other two (my friends and rivals
for the girl who was chosen to be Mary)
never faltered with frankincense and myrrh.

Now that was a long time ago.
And now I know them for what they were,
moving across vague spaces on their camels,
visionaries, madmen, poor creatures possessed
by some slight deviation of the stars.
I know their gifts were shabby, if symbolic.
Their wisdom was a thing of waking dreams.
Their robes were dirty and their breath was bad.

Still, I would dream them back.
Let them be wooden and absurd again
in all the painted glory that a child
loved. Let me be one of them.
Let me step forward once more awkwardly
and stammer and choke on my prepared speech.
I will bring gold again and kneel
foolish and adoring in the dungy straw.

THE CAGE

Take, then, this image for what it's worth:
the eagle that I saw once, loved where he poised,
a sad brown thing roosting like a hen on a pole.
He was, of course, a captive. It was the zoo.
The cage was round and domed and let in light
and some of the jigsawed blue of the sky.
(I was a boy then. Love was fiercely caged.)

Outside there were peacocks on the grass.
They strutted on the clipped lawn like
elegant ancestors, folding and unfolding
intricate fans adorned with flaming eyes.
He was alone with scattered winks of sky,
the broken weather. Bald as a monk,
he seldom moved from his perch, never flew,

though there was room enough. He waited.
Sometimes he would stir, open his huge wings.
Then, *you thought, seeing the beak, cruel talons,*
and the shadows of his wings like twin sails,
that nothing made of iron could keep him.
But that was just a whim, a ghostly gesture.
He wouldn't eat and so he died.

Afterwards there were still peacocks to look at,
and the small birds in their delicate cages,
and rare ones with beaks and coloring to prove
God has a sense of humor in some climates.
But chiefly there was the cage like a great wound,
like an eye put out, like space where a tree has been.
Wind sang in that empty place and you wanted to pray.

THE GRAPES

In Tuscany
where I was a soldier for a while
the grapes were wonderful on hillsides.
They grew and glistened in the light.
They dreamed all season long
the tuneful dreams of Tuscany.

And they clotted & clustered & swelled
and they spilled over like fountains
green & shining everywhere you looked

until in tidal waves they broke
over the stranded barbwire
flooding pillboxes foxholes & minefields

stalling tanks & trucks
disrupting wire communications
and even carried away the CP tent.

By Christ we got drunk!
We drank and drank
and drank the blood
    of Tuscany.

And reeling in that holy light
    of Tuscany
we dreamed that all the towers leaned
    in Tuscany.

DEEP SEA FISHING

Why we were fishing there I can't remember.
There was the boat, idle and white, freshly painted.
There was a whole boatload of us, absurd in the clothes
that tourists, like pilgrims, tend to wear,
dropping our thin dark lines into a sea like smoke,
and calm, too, not the least wind to scale it.
And our bright hooks, cruel and baited, faded
out of sight, concealed in fires of mystery.

What were we seeking? Treasure, I guess,
danced for the young men like a veiled girl.
There was an old woman in black. Maybe she hoped
to seize the hushed bones of a lover, drowned.
Others longed for small things—a watch, a ring,
perhaps a bottle with a message in it or,
at least, some noble question. For the children,
I believe, any marvel would have pleased.

I remember we fished all day without a stroke
of luck. The men began to swear and stamp the deck
and wish for wind. The old woman leaned against the rail
and let her tears fall in the sea like alms. Just then,
as the sun went down and a light breeze stirred up waves,
there were the mermaids, half of deep sea and
half of mortal flesh, out there in the late dazzle
of pure gold singing and singing and singing.

"Quick!" Cried the captain, starting the engine
like a roaring lion. We turned for shore.
Lines were hauled in or thrown away for good,
and we left them flashing in our ghostly wake,
thrashing in the fury of our swift farewell.
Some held their ears, while others shook their fists.
Some cursed, some prayed, and someone blew a kiss.
The children sang awhile and then forgot the tune.

EVE

I like the version of Aristophanes,
the story he tells in the Symposium,
how we were altogether once and how,
ripped apart, uncoupled, sundered,
we are the lost and naked halves,
and how we dream of that wholeness
as, say, a man who's lost a leg
sometimes feels the joy of his missing limb
springing, dancing, running . . .
and other times he feels it longing
to belong to him again. I don't know
which of these is the greater torment.

The other story, how in dreamy Eden
Adam lost a rib without a wound
and woke to find a stranger he could love,
is too stern for the banquet scene.
I was there. Stood in that garden.
I named the birds, the beasts, the trees.
I tasted the joys of that forbidden apple.
I remember the core was bitter in my mouth
and when I spat the seeds they grew into barbwire.
I heard the thunder of God's kettle drums.
Wounded then, at last, I took your hand.
And we are still together.

BAYONET DRILL

TIME: Winter
PLACE: Camp Chaffee, Arkansas

In new fatigues the young recruits
form beside a wooden stand.
The sergeant holds the weapon up,
blued and heavy in his hand.

The wind cuts deep in Arkansas.
They stamp their boots and huddle close.
He points to where the victims wait—
two ranks of men of straw.

First they'll drill, first must learn
long thrust, short thrust, neat butt strokes;
at his command must jump and shout
until their hoarse throats burn.

Then, worn out, dirty, they must be
sent charging through the scarecrow ranks
to pierce the hearts and crack the skulls
of this first man-sized enemy.

He holds it up by the grooved hilt,
noting the beauty, the balance of
the tapered lines and its fine point.
Someone giggles from a sense of guilt,

giving occasion in the still
hush following for him to snap:
"Nothing to laugh at! A bayonet
has just one purpose—that's to kill."

They eye the death he handles, feel
suddenly their chill guts knot and tumble.
The straw men dance in the dusty wind
indifferent to keen weather and cold steel.

65

EPISODE IN A SUBURBAN GARDEN

In full pursuit of parallels
I am arrested at the outset
of a trembling May morning
to hear the birds compete.

Gardens are smaller now,
are echoes of the fragrant time
when suns ploughed up the zodiac
and minds were overwhelmed

by vivid signals. Music
of the eclectic flowers can
be fully apprehended
only by a private eye.

But all the birds are singing
to confound the register.
Even the poorest blossoms reel,
intoxicated and colorful.

One might annihilate philosophy
here and now. One might reduce
the beautiful and inconsistent gods
to narrow gauge.

What stupidity! When I
should be naked and listening,
no more than an eye, an ear,
I respond to innocence

with violence. How easily
accomplishment becomes a fault.
The heart like an empty glove
gropes awkwardly for love.

THREE DANCERS

I saw a tall rider on a dark horse.
He sat straight up and down in the saddle
while the horse, reined in taut, was stamping
his shadow to pieces.

I've seen a girl in a swing, her body
arched against bright sky, her hair,
her flesh shining. She was ringing
her blood with joy like a bell.

I've seen an old man shake his fist
in a storm as if the sky were glass
and he could break it with a bloody fist.
As if the storm were himself.

I remember all three. I remember
the young girl singing her blood
and the old man cursing the day of his.
But chiefly I remember

the proud horseman and the dance
of the dark horse, the holy dance
of blood to bit and spur while he
trampled a shadow to death.

BATHING BEAUTY

The sun, this morning
scored for trumpets, blares
over the sculptured gestures of
bathers in bright costumes.

They are untouched.
Only gulls and children fly
for pure joy to the holy noise.
Older we warm by the tune

like the blind by a roaring
fire. Cat-sleek, curled
in knowledge of herself,
dozing in the dazzle,

she has caught my eye.
I see her on a scallop shell
or lounging in the perfect lines
of a Matisse.

O Suzanna, I'll
stand on tiptoes, breathless
among the frozen elders. O
Judith, here's my head

my heart my four limbs
and my balls and all
(O Ruth) my alien corn.
She stretches, sighs, and seems

to be asleep. I shut my eyes
to hear the gulls and children
sing. I hear my voice
wailing by an ancient wall.

The sun, all trumpets, blares
and the sea is falling, falling
like the walls of Jericho
whose waves are tongues of dust.

LETTER FROM A LIGHT DRINKER

"You cannot suck poetry out of the cosmos with a straw."

—A. E. Friedman

One time in the Army I was poor,
too poor even to buy a postage stamp,
a razor blade, a toothpaste tube.
(It happens like that once in a while.)

I had a buddy who would stand me to
a single can of beer at five o'clock.
Dusty, dirty from working, I'd run
all the way from Motor Pool to EM Club.

The thing to do was to sip it through a straw.
It made the beer last longer and
bubbles rose, shining, dancing, in your brain,
and I'm telling you (you better believe it)

the world turned upside down and glowed.
You might as well have been in China
or in Thule where (they say) ice jewels everything
and on clear nights you can hear the stars

make lucid fugues like a hive of bells.
It was good, it was fine, and I've never been
drunker or happier since and more dazed,
ravished by the riches of this world

or more fearful of my diet in the next.

SNOWSTORM

Snow fell everywhere equally and froze
everything moving. The trees gave up the ghost
and took a hush of whiteness in their arms.
The small birds flying, caught in charms
of cold, remained in constellations in the sky.
The world, so sown with chill, shone like a trophy.

This is a time for students of excess:
the nude of dreams perpetually undressed,
the sight and aim of hunter fixed
on the beast he follows, but no trick
or magic lets him find the mark,
nor scholar sign a footnote to his work.

These things born in fire now take the cure
of ice, reside, contemplative and poor,
in cells of singleness. Secret as prayer,
no inner voices ring in open air,
no music finds a form when, like a spell,
the cold has cracked the heart of every bell.

Safe is the sleeping beauty never kissed.
Safe are the ghostly trees, secure from risk
of all green winds and singing birds.
And safe the hero from all speeches and awards.
Only the scholar's left to mourn the cost,
the rigor paid for wonder and for loss.

THE SLEEPING GYPSY

AND OTHER POEMS

BY GEORGE GARRETT

With drawings by Jo ALYS DOWNS

HAS BEEN COMPOSED IN TEN POINT INTERTYPE WAVERLEY, LEADED
FOUR POINTS, PRINTED LITHOGRAPH ON CHILLICOTHE LOGAN EGGSHELL
PAPER, BOUND IN DUPONT CRAFTSMAN PX BINDING CLOTH BY THE
UNIVERSITY OF TEXAS PRINTING DIVISION, AND PUBLISHED AS A SUPPLE-
MENT TO VOLUME ONE, NUMBER TWO OF *The Texas Quarterly* BY THE
UNIVERSITY OF TEXAS PRESS